THE BERLIN WALL

D0405200

View of the border between East and West Berlin with the
Brandenburg Gate, seen from the Reichstag. At the lower edge of
the picture, the painted Western side of the Wall backed by a
watchtower. To the right of the Brandenburg Gate, the white
Western side of the second wall.
Photo 1988, Manfred Hamm

The Wall in Kreuzberg at Bethaniendamm/Adalbertstrasse.
In the background, the church, Thomaskirche, and Mariannenplatz.
Photo 1985, Hermann Waldenburg

Border installations at Zimmerstrasse, near Friedrichstrasse and Checkpoint Charlie. In the foreground, the Wall with Keith Haring and part of his 325-foot-long graffiti from 1986.
Photo 1986, House at Checkpoint Charlie

YOU ARE LEAVING
THE AMERICAN SECTOR
ВЫ ВЫЕЗЖАЕТЕ ИЗ
АМЕРИКАНСКОГО СЕКТОРА
VOUS SORTEZ
DU SECTEUR AMÉRICAIN
SIE VERLASSEN DEN AMERIKANISCHEN SEKTOR

THE BERLIN WALL

Photographs and Introduction
Hermann Waldenburg

Abbeville Press · Publishers · New York

Cover illustration:
Christophe Bouchet and Michael Gremenz
Design: Hermann Waldenburg
Cover design: Debbie Glasserman
Illustrations in the chronology of events:
Landesbildstelle Berlin (5), Zenit (1),
House at Checkpoint Charlie (6)
Translation: Ann Robertson

Library of Congress Cataloging-in-Publication Data
Waldenburg, Hermann, 1940–
    The Berlin Wall/photographs and introduction, Hermann
  Waldenburg.
        p.   cm.
    ISBN 1-55859-131-1
    1. Mural painting and decoration — Berlin (Germany) 2. Mural
  painting and decoration — 20th century — Berlin (Germany)
  3. Graffiti — Berlin (Germany) 4. Street art — Berlin (Germany)
  5. Berlin wall (1961–   ) 6. Berlin (Germany) — Buildings, structures,
  etc. I. Title.
  ND2751.B4W35   1990   90-729
  751.7'3'09431554 — dc20   CIP

First American edition

Nothing is so bad that it does not also
bear within it the seed of something good
(Chinese saying)

My recollection of the Berlin Wall before the end of 1984 is as blurred as a line spray-painted from too great a distance. My memory resembles the state of the Wall in February 1990: holes and gaps, the surface layer skinned, with the upper edge alone carrying reminders through the remains of graffiti, shreds of images, islands of color.

"Wall of shame"—"Anti-fascist bulwark." Those were the antithetical projections of West and East during the Cold War. How many attempts, ending in death, were made to overcome the Wall? So much tunneling, scaling, vaulting, flying over, ramming, and crashing through. When was the rough breeze-block construction, crowned with barbed wire, replaced by prefabricated concrete slabs slotted into iron supports? Did this version already have the smooth piping on top? Whatever its form, the Wall always represented an inhuman rift in the lives of the Berliners. My awareness of it was influenced more by the media than by everyday restrictions: standard reports of successful escapes, headlines about orders to shoot; news items, statistics.

I moved to Berlin in March 1961. What was the current semi-official status tag in those days? Was Berlin the capital, the former capital, a four-sector city, Berlin (West), Berlin-West, West Berlin? How long did it reign as the frontier city, or the showcase of the West, or the turntable between East and West? Whatever the case, it was a special unit, conscription-free, a metropolis. When the border was erected on August 13, I was in Norway on an island. When I returned, West Berlin was an island, surrounded by a Wall, barbed wire, and "GDR." "Don't you feel walled-in in the divided city?"

In 1968 I moved to Kreuzberg, next to the Wall. Were there any "daubings" then? The Wall couldn't have been attractive. It was an area of negative emotions. On the East, there were watchtowers with border guards, rifles shouldered, field glasses alert, straightfaced. On the Western side, patrols with MPs in open jeeps, Berlin police in bunkers. With an occasional smile, the Westerners tried to prevent attempts at arson; attacks with explosives; provocateurs or drunks trying to climb the Wall; suicides by car drivers; happenings; actions; environments; installations at or using the Wall. Evidence of any success was rapidly and thoroughly eradicated. After all, this was a German Wall and it had to be kept clean. The rear, socialist side was hermetically sealed off anyway and spotlessly white, except temporarily after a few bloody incidents. By contrast, when I was in Rome from 1973 to 1974, I was amazed at the abundance of painted and sprayed political slogans. House walls, garden walls, bridges, all were covered with written symbols, often superimposed: *Vota si*—*Vota no; Jesus si*—*Superstar no.* Were these influenced by the wall newspapers of the Chinese Cultural Revolution, which we were crazy about in those days? Or simply parts of the Roman heritage?

In Berlin the extraparliamentary scriptural struggle of the '68 generation took place more in the city itself, at the university, in and on public buildings. Down with …, Freedom for …, Victory to …, Death to …, Long live he, she, it …. The Wall was too distant for all this, except for a few demonstration points: Bernauer Strasse, the Brandenburg Gate, Potsdamer Platz. Potsdamer Platz was where anti-American slogans were quickly blotted out an hour before President Jimmy Carter visited the Wall. Political—and later, private—convictions, personal and collective opinions, materialized as slogans, signs, and emblems. They forced their way into public awareness as posters, wall stickers and leaflets, masks (during the Shah's visit), boards and banners, flags, streamers, and on clothes and costumes. Paints and brushes were among the many media employed, usually during nighttime escapades; the spray can was either not yet in fashion or too expensive. The various messages on the Wall were relatively unsophisticated, sometimes simple: GDR = KZ (concentration camp); USA = SA/SS; someone felt he was being pursued, persecuted by alien transmitters, and meticulously noted it down; short prose was featured (Maria, I love you). Paintings of a ladder or a door (entrance fee 1 mark) were obvious symbols.

A new and different quality was introduced by the unpolitical(?) activity of Harald Nägeli, the Zurich Sprayer. His linear figures, exclusively in spray-paint technique, inspired the creative instincts of all those whom Joseph Beuys and Andy Warhol had previously encouraged to do their own thing: Everyone is an artist! Everything is beautiful! Nägeli — sentenced to jail in Switzerland, wanted by Interpol, courted with a professorship in Wiesbaden — exemplified the broad spectrum in which a bright mixture of desires toward artistic and self-expression started to flourish in the eighties. Another major influence also came from outside. New York graffiti became known in Europe; in 1984 a book entitled *Subway Art* was published in England. The colorful technique employed in this new art form was aerosol spraying. New York teenagers had already discovered it at the beginning of the seventies. At first used on walls in the local neighborhoods as a form of basic self-expression — signatures, pseudonyms, monograms (tags) — the spray-can then received its full subcultural initiation on the subway cars. Some users of this speedy and effective technique (writers) gained recognition with their written artwork (pieces), sometimes even at the top end of the art market.

Thus many things combined to discover a common medium in Berlin, unique to the world: The Wall. In its fourth improved edition, it now had almost seamless joins; its surface was smooth, weatherproof, and — at first — painted white. Perfectionism and an obsession for cleanliness created not only the world's securest border system, but also an ideal ground for emulsions and lacquers.

I don't recall exactly when this fifteen-foot-high and 102-mile-long painting area started to fill up. Was it 1982, '83, '84? In the meantime, the Wall and its adjacent car-free strip had become a hot spot for walking and cycling freaks, intermingled with alternative tourists. While most of the city on the Western side was being built up and the last traces of the war were disappearing, this area still offered ruins, decaying historic buildings, wildly overgrown wasteland, pavements and road surfaces dating back to the thirties and forties. The Tempodrome, the Rollheimer Settlement (an ad hoc collection of often imaginative homes), the Martin Gropius Building (a museum and exhibition center), the Künstlerhaus Bethanien (a cultural and community center in a disused hospital) — all brought life and liveliness into the immediate vicinity of the Wall.

After the summer recess in 1984, I read on some red-green multicolored steps leading up to the Wall near the Martin Gropius Building: "More beer, more meat, less Orwell. God ble$$ 1984." To the left and right were various anthropoid fantasy figures whose favorite pursuit seemed to lie in merry gesticulations. Was all this intended as a serious warning, or was it giving an ironic "all clear" in the face of Orwell's macabre prophecy? In any event, the sudden perception of this multifigured fantasy world held a special meaning for me. At the time, I was pondering an inaugural lecture with which to commence teaching at a school for communication design. The nature and context of the Wall art seemed to typify a basic understanding of this special field of activity, which is a prime constituent of our media world. Nothing characterizes it better than the formula developed by the American political scientist Harold D. Lasswell in 1948: "Who Says What in Which Channel to Whom with What Effects?" I bought a camera, the first in my life. During the winter of 1984/85 I photographed the best and most interesting paintings for my lecture. There was a huge selection between Potsdamer Platz and Mariannenplatz. If I had known how quickly they were to disappear again, I would have used up a dozen more rolls of film. After my lecture in June 1985, I regularly visited "my" pictures — armed with my camera — to see how they had changed, or whether they had disappeared, to be replaced by new ones. I made my shots through the eyes of a painter, concentrating on subjectively selected details. The whole adventure was like a substitute occupation for me, for professionally I had moved away from painting and turned to furniture and object design. The slides documented independent and applied art, which I transposed to a different medium and a particular format; there was rarely a long shot of the Wall, and never a picture of the artist or the public.

Who created this communication for everyman, free of charge, by day and night? The Wall was well illuminated for the display of its fruits. Three signatures occurred regularly: Faux pas, Bouchet, and Noir. At that time they seemed to me to be the most imaginative, inventive, and productive of the painters. Were they the first to work on large areas? Certainly, they sometimes covered hundreds of yards.

Their styles were recognizable. Some of Bouchet's faces had a smile, as if they recognized me too. But there were many, equally talented, anonymous artists who displayed a completely different, characteristic hand in their use of color and form. Everyone can discover them for themselves in this book, just as I once discovered them, and grow to like or dislike them. Names were not important. I had no scientific interest in the pictures and their authors. Their spontaneous honesty, their personal uniqueness really inspired me. It didn't matter who'd been at work, whether a graffiti pro or a simpleton, a dilettantish polit-freak, art students, an inadvertently brilliant amateur, an ambitious teenager, a hobby artist rising above himself, or even tourists — they were all the same to me and equally unknown.

Rarely did I see a painter at work. One thing is clear: The artists didn't belong to a single age or social group: emigrants and immigrants from Eastern Europe and South America, Swiss and Scots, French and West Berliners, North Friesians on a weekend trip — and Americans who had been invited and concluded their visit with a press conference (Keith Haring, 1986). They all shared the ever-decreasing free areas in peacefully creative competition. Once, someone came along and stormed the whole picture show. A former citizen of East Germany, he demonstratively shattered all pleasant outward appearances by drawing a brutal, continuous white line with a paint-roller, chest-high along the Wall; he went on for miles until he was finally caught by waiting GDR border guards: six months' jail for willful damage to "the People's property." As a kind of involuntary concept art or minimal art, the line remained visible for a time; but it was soon used for inscriptions, and pictures were retouched. By 1988 at the latest it had completely disappeared again under new images.

"What we want can't be bought" was a statement written on a wall that had itself been painted on the Wall. A large section appeared to have been detonated out of the real Wall, as well as from the second wall painted in the background. On the death-strip between the two, a small child was depicted flying a kite. "Death to Tyrants!" was written around an ambivalent sign that compressed hammer and sickle, stars and stripes into concentric circles. And: "Berlin will be WALL-free." This last message was unambiguous, and it wasn't long before it became reality. Other words on the Wall articulated appeals to, desires for, fears of, joy at, longing for: "Hunger, Your Reverence" — "Only those who move feel their chains" — "Power is always loveless, love never powerless." Here were wish fulfillment dreams, aggressive and angry, sad and ironic, gay and wily! "I like Beuys/(boys)" — "The Wall must stay" — "Concrete makes you happy" — "Shit" — "Come on over and join the party!" — "Bern greets Berlin." Sometimes Wall poetry, sometimes proverbial ("a white wall is a fool's writing paper"), sometimes simply a form of "I was here." While Wolfgang Neuss created a lengthy and superbly amusing reading out of this writing on the Wall, I concentrated less on the inscriptions: I was on a picture hunt. To me, the pictures represented apt translations of public opinions into a color and sign language: the *vox populi*, the voice of the people, in visual form. There were wise sayings, inanities, daydreams enciphered in human figures, faces, skeletons, landscapes, animals. Comiclike in structure and statement: "God wants cash" — "Heroin out" — "Pirate art"; but also the pure pleasure in free form, in creating; in smudging, daubing, inventing. There were many echoes of twentieth-century art trends, but rather than being imitated or directly reproduced, as is common among pavement artists, they were creatively adapted. A heterogeneous amalgam — uninhibited, partisan, not nostalgic like all the "neo" movements seen in museums and galleries — produced a new popular art form, a new art. Was it perhaps the major art phenomenon of the eighties, to be ranked with the new trends in furniture and object design? Precisely because it did not pretend to be anything brilliantly ostentatious, did not demand labels or high prices, it was an expression of *zeitgeist*, the spirit of the times. This grass roots art reflected contemporary movements and, if only until the next image was superimposed, bore witness to current political events. The Wall told the history of the times: in succession, the Republic of free Wendland — squatters' movement — breakdance — dying forests — Tunix (do nothing movement) — Tuwat (do something movement) — PEACE.

To whom did all this say something? Whom did it please? Who turned red with anger? I didn't ask or count them, but their numbers increased. The world's longest painting developed into a pilgrim route, a way of the Cross through the city for mass tourism. The particular stations: Reichstag, Brandenburg Gate, Potsdamer Platz, Stresemann/Hubertusstrasse, Friedrichstrasse, Leuschnerdamm, Bethaniendamm, Mariannenplatz. A coming and going, seeing and spraying, photographing, in the city with the best-preserved city wall. Was it the eighth world wonder? By 1987 the Wall was full, with no more good free spaces to be had anywhere, not even in Wedding, Reinickendorf, Neukölln. Everyone had something to say to everyone now: the early pensioner, the late migrant, the neighborhood kids, the anonymous alcoholic, and the famous artist. Only the East Berliners were excluded, and, of course, those men in their gray-green uniforms on permanent lookout too. That was bound to make curiosity grow.

How had it been possible to attract hundreds of thousands through simple painting? Despite, or precisely because of the digitalized, animated, flickering flood of electronic media monitors, huge numbers allowed themselves to be jerked out of their role as passive recipients to become active participants. The amazement at what could be done with paint and brush, the secret attraction of the forbidden, but also the urge to change the unchangeable, gave many the impulse to communicate visually, something they had never before had the confidence to do. Brushes, small and large, painted and stubbed over the concrete surface, freehand or with adhesive tape, which gave sharper contours. The use of spray-paint demanded a certain amount of expertise. It meant working rapidly and at the correct distance; direct mixing wasn't possible. This influenced the general appearance: clear bright colors; flowing, animated lines and forms; a type of cell-technique usually with black outlines. Spray-can graffiti were the real technical and stylistic innovation, a separate chapter in art history. Prepared stencils made of paper, cardboard, and tin were a useful aid in speeding up the reproduction of inscriptions and images on the Wall. Stencil art, nothing new, was brought to new fruition; it could be sprayed, painted, or rolled on. Felt-tip, chalk, pencil, lipstick — everything was possible, except scraping and scratching, which was difficult because of the hardness of the material. There were forms of illusionist painting, collages, wallpaperings, poster and copy art; occasionally there were mosaics, material, and object installations. The Wall was a temporary museum. The demands in the sixties for the "democratization" of art and culture, the reduction of psychological barriers, the opening of the "temples of the muses," were all met here. Everyone was allowed to touch, to participate at will, to demonstrate directly approval or disapproval. A visual dialogue began.

What can be said about the results? The suggestive profusion of color and images on the surface produced a sense of high pressure, the bleak white emptiness of the base, an inner vacuum. This mottled wall could no longer be taken seriously. Was this panopticon really supposed to stand for another hundred years, as the GDR leader Erich Honecker maintained? Ludicrous — implosion was bound to occur, as it did on November 9, 1989. Had art developed a revolutionary force and effect for the first time?

What is bound to fall, must be toppled, as Karl Marx once stated. The Wall still stands, though riddled with holes. The images have fallen, have been hacked into minute, even minuscule pieces and carried off in jacket pockets and plastic bags. Decollage? Souvenir hunt? Vandalism? When something comes to an end there is usually a retrospective. Berlin's graffiti, its Wall Art, developed from rather meager beginnings into the tentative experimentation of the seventies and reached its zenith between 1983 and 1986. It became a powerfully expressive, flat, posterlike, popular art form that will take its place in this century's annals. In a way, it was a self-mutating phenomenon, a process of superimposition, deletion, adaptation. The innovative power and artistic potential were soon exhausted. At first, the pictures were without signatures, now there were signatures without pictures. Rudimentary self-expression became an overinflated end in itself: "tags" and "pieces" along American lines, second- and third-hand copies occasionally executed with European finesse. Nägeli is said to have drawn a comparison with the stationing of new American Pershing rockets. Now and again I continued to discover small delicacies in remote districts and photographed them. After a few days, they too would be destroyed again by amateur and professional "Wall-Woodpeckers," sold off, given away, made into tiepins, or mounted on pieces of wood with barbed wire trimmings. Keepsakes, mementos.

This is a "picture-book" dedicated to the artists.

35   1985

41   1985

109   1989

Cordoning off the Brandenburg Gate, August 1961.

Construction of a stronger wall in the district of Wedding, August 1963

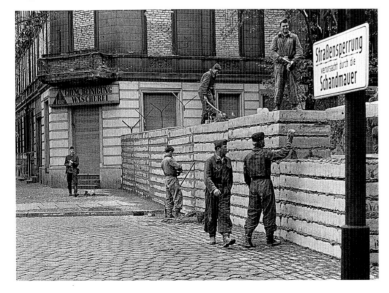

1961

MARCH 13   President John F. Kennedy reaffirmed the determination of the United States to protect the freedom of Berlin.

JUNE 3-4   President Kennedy and Soviet premier Nikita Khrushchev met in Vienna, where grave differences on the question of Germany and Berlin became apparent.

JULY/AUGUST   The number of refugees from East Berlin and the GDR rapidly increased. Some 2,000 people per day came over to West Berlin between August 1 and 12. East Germany announced the preparation of "measures to safeguard the security of the German Democratic Republic."

AUGUST 13   In the early hours of this Sunday morning, units of the People's Police and the National People's Army of the GDR began blocking off the Eastern sector from the three Western sectors. Two days later, the construction of a concrete wall began. The border guards received orders to shoot. Deaths occurred among refugees attempting escape.

AUGUST 23   Only seven crossing points remained allowing access between East and West Berlin. The GDR government declared that only West Berliners holding a special permit would be allowed access to the East. As issuing procedures failed, it was impossible for West Berliners to visit the East.

1962

JANUARY 24   Twenty-eight men, women, and children managed to escape to West Berlin through a tunnel built under the Wall.

JUNE 8   Fourteen East Berliners seized a passenger ferry and escaped across the River Spree under a hail of bullets from GDR border guards. They reached the West Berlin bank unharmed.

AUGUST 17   Eighteen-year-old Peter Fechter was caught by bullets during an escape attempt. Seriously wounded, he was left lying near the Wall on East Berlin territory, where he bled to death.

President John F. Kennedy at the Brandenburg Gate, blanketed with red drapes, June 26, 1963.

The Wall in the mid-sixties.

1963

JUNE 26   President Kennedy visited Berlin and expressed his solidarity with the West Berliners in a now legendary speech. He concluded with the words: "All free men, wherever they may live, are citizens of Berlin, and therefore, as a free man, I take pride in the words: *Ich bin ein Berliner*."

DECEMBER 17   An agreement on the issue of border–crossing permits, effective from December 19 until January 5, enabled West Berliners to visit relatives in the Eastern part of the city for the first time since the border was closed.

1964

OCTOBER 5   In the greatest tunnel escape since the Wall was erected, fifty-seven East Berliners successfully reached the Western part of the city.

1970

MARCH 19   West Germany's chancellor, Willy Brandt, and the chairman of the GDR Council of Ministers, Willi Stoph, met in Erfurt, East Germany.

MARCH 26   The US, Great Britain, France and the Soviet Union started negotiations on a Berlin Agreement.

1971

JANUARY 31   Reestablishment of telephone communications, which had been cut since 1952.

MAY 3   Walter Ulbricht resigned from office as general secretary of the Central Committee of the Socialist Unity party, to be replaced by Erich Honecker.

SEPTEMBER 3   The ambassadors to the Federal Republic of Germany representing the US, Great Britain, and France and the Soviet ambassador to the GDR signed the Quadripartite Agreement on Berlin. The agreement regulated free access to West Berlin and guaranteed the maintenance and development of ties between West Berlin and the Federal Republic.

The Wall and a border guard, August 21, 1963.

An abortive escape attempt by bus.

1972

DECEMBER 21   West German minister Egon Bahr and GDR State Secretary Michael Kohl met in East Berlin to sign the Basic Agreement on Relationships between the Federal Republic and the German Democratic Republic.

1975

OCTOBER 29   Agreement between the GDR and the West Berlin Senate on mutual assistance in the case of accidents on border waterways.

1980

OCTOBER 9   The GDR authorities raised the compulsory payment for visitors from West Berlin and the Federal Republic of Germany to twenty-five deutsche marks per day.

1982

JUNE 11   President Ronald Reagan visited West Berlin during a tour of Europe. In a speech outlining the so-called Berlin Initiative he summoned the Soviet Union to take cooperative steps toward the securing of peace.

1984

JANUARY 20   Six GDR citizens applied for political asylum at the US Embassy in East Berlin. They were allowed to cross to West Berlin two days later.

JANUARY 24   Twelve GDR citizens sought refuge at the Permanent Representation of the Federal Republic in East Berlin. They, too, were granted exit to West Berlin.

MARCH 14   GDR border guards erected a second wall between the Brandenburg Gate and Potsdamer Platz. Since its construction in August 1961, the Wall had already claimed seventy-three lives.

The Wall at Potsdamer Platz, 1974.

President Ronald Reagan at the Brandenburg Gate, June 12, 1987.

1985

MARCH 11 Mikhail Gorbachev elected as the new secretary general of the Communist party in the Soviet Union.

1987

JUNE 7–8 A rock concert was held in front of the Reichstag in West Berlin and many teenagers also congregated on the Eastern side of the Wall in order to listen. There was conflict on the Eastern side with the People's Police and members of the State Security Service. About a thousand teenagers chanted, "The Wall must go!"

JUNE 12 During Berlin's 750th anniversary celebrations, President Reagan visited the city. In a speech in front of the Brandenburg Gate he said, "The Wall cannot withstand freedom."

DECEMBER 10 GDR security forces prevented a demonstration in East Berlin organized by the domestic "Initiative for Peace and Human Rights."

1988

JANUARY In East Berlin numerous members of peace and human rights' groups were arrested. There and in many other towns of East Germany people congregated in prayers of appeal each evening.

1989

JANUARY 18 Honecker declared that the Wall would "remain for fifty, even a hundred years, as long as the reasons for its building remain."

FEBRUARY 6 A young man was shot dead at the Wall by border guards while trying to escape. He was the last in a total of seventy-nine victims to die there before the borders were finally opened nine months later.

MARCH 8 A thirty-two-year-old GDR citizen crashed to his death in the West Berlin district of Zehlendorf in an attempt to escape in a self-made hot-air balloon.

A section of the new Wall at the Brandenburg Gate, 1976.

People at the Wall, November 10, 1989.

MAY 7   Local elections in East Germany resulted in protests and allegations of fraud.

JUNE 7   In East Berlin, after a protest demonstration against fraudulent practice during the local elections, some 120 citizens were temporarily held in custody.

AUGUST 8   By now 131 GDR citizens had sought refuge and refused to leave the Permanent Representation of the Federal Republic in East Berlin. The building had to be closed because of overcrowding.

AUGUST 19   During a cultural event on the Hungarian-Austrian border, approximately 900 GDR citizens took the opportunity and made a mass escape to West Germany via Austria. Since August 1, more than 3,000 GDR citizens had escaped via Hungary. In the following weeks the number of people taking this escape route increased.

SEPTEMBER 11   Hungary opened the border to Austria. By the end of the month about 10,000 GDR citizens had crossed through Austria into West Germany. Founding of the "New Forum" in East Berlin by critics of the GDR regime.

OCTOBER 7   In East Berlin, official ceremonies celebrated the fortieth anniversary of the GDR. Thousands demonstrated there and in other East German cities for democracy and freedom of opinion. Soviet State and Party chief Mikhail Gorbachev openly exhorted the GDR leadership to enter into the reform process and warned, "Life punishes those who come too late."

OCTOBER 9   Mass demonstration in Leipzig, with 70,000 participants. Among the slogans: "We Are the People!"

OCTOBER 18   After eighteen years in power as State and Party chief, Erich Honecker was forced out of office. The Socialist Unity party Central Committee elected Egon Krenz as successor. Krenz announced imminent reforms.

OCTOBER 21–30   Hundreds of thousands participated in demonstrations that swept East Berlin and other major towns and cities in East Germany.

The newly opened Wall at Potsdamer Platz, November 12, 1989.

New Year's celebrations at the Brandenburg Gate, December 31, 1989.

NOVEMBER 4   A protest rally against the Socialist Unity party regime was staged at Alexanderplatz in East Berlin. Over this particular weekend, some 15,000 GDR citizens arrived in West Germany via Czechoslovakia.

NOVEMBER 7   Resignation of the GDR government, followed next day by the resignation of the entire Politburo. Increasing demonstrations and floods of refugees.

NOVEMBER 9   In the evening, the GDR government unexpectedly opened the borders to the Federal Republic and West Berlin. Throughout the night tens of thousands streamed through the Wall into West Berlin.

NOVEMBER 10   Dismantling of the Wall commenced by GDR border guards to create new crossing points. East and West Berliners joined in the dismantling process.

NOVEMBER 11-12   During this weekend three million GDR citizens visited West Germany to take a look, go shopping, and visit friends and relatives. Tens of thousands came to West Berlin, filling the Kurfürstendamm and inner city.

NOVEMBER 13   The People's Parliament of the GDR elected Hans Modrow, former Socialist Unity party leader in Dresden, new prime minister. In Leipzig more than 200,000 people demonstrated again for political reforms. The "Monday demonstrations" continued in Leipzig and other East German cities during the following weeks.

DECEMBER 3   Resignation of the entire Socialist Unity party leadership under Egon Krenz. Former State and Party chief Erich Honecker was expelled from the party along with a series of other leading communist functionaries.

DECEMBER 22   The Brandenburg Gate, for twenty-eight years a symbol of German division, was reopened to pedestrians.

DECEMBER 31   Some 500,000 people, including visitors from all over the world, joined in New Year's celebrations at the Brandenburg Gate.

Nowhere in Europe was the division between East and West so visible and palpable as in Berlin.

For twenty-eight years, two months, and twenty-six days, a bastion of concrete walls and wire fences divided the city — and the world — in two. The blockade of the East against the three Western sectors of Berlin began on August 13, 1961. After August 15, the barbed wire roadblocks were replaced by a wall. Over the years the barrier was continuously "perfected": a new wall made of concrete slabs, at places up to fifteen feet high, was built and backed up by a series of security installations along a strip more than 325 feet wide. Round the whole of West Berlin there thus developed a 102-mile-long border system consisting of walls, fences, alarms, tank traps, dog runs, trip wires, ditches and pits, searchlights, automatic shooting devices, forty-three bunkers, and 295 watchtowers. The border guards had orders to shoot any escapees. Up until November 9, when the wall was opened, seventy-nine people died during escape attempts in Berlin.

Hermann Waldenburg was born in 1940 in Waldenburg, Germany (now in Poland). He studied art and graphic design at the Folkwang School of Art in Essen, the Art Academy at Stuttgart, and the High School of Arts in West Berlin. He has worked as an independent artist and graphic designer in Berlin since 1967 and as a furniture and object designer since 1982. He has been professor of design at the School of Art in Augsburg since 1984.